Kudos for *Cookies...*

"The concept that Russ shares in Cookies is useful ONLY if *(1)* you have teammates who are afraid to prospect, or *(2)* you yourself have ever been afraid to prospect. The training in this book will melt your fears just like the delicious chocolate chips in the amazing cookies served inside."

—*Ray Higdon, #1 earner, blogger*

"The painter of parables, Russ McNeil, has done it again. *The Most Expensive Cookies in the World* is a quick, easy read, and packed with powerful points that can benefit network marketers of every level. This book should definitely be in ever networker's library!"

—*Rod Nichols, Successful team-builder and Author of* The Twelve Power Secrets for Network Marketing Success

---

"Only 2 words come to mind with Russ McNeil: *prolific* and *profound*. He has done it again with a book that will rock your world. The 'Cookies Book' is about as powerful as any book I've read in years. Readers should have their 'Cookie Journals' in front of them in order to take notes. Radically brilliant! Don't just read it—consume it!!!"

—*Doug Firebaugh, CEO, PassionFire International,* www.PassionFire.com

---

"*The Most Expensive Cookies in the World* is really fun, it's easy to read, and it draws you into the story to make you feel like you're actually participating! *Cookies* is full of tasty morsels that grab your attention quickly; felt like I was eating those chocolate chip cookies hot, right out of the oven, melting in my mouth and craving more! Anyone can use this training book to build their business without gaining a single pound! I highly recommend *Cookies* to all networking connoisseurs and their apprentices! Kudos, again to Russ for another irresistible contribution to our profession!"

—*Sue Seward, The Gluten Free Lady*

"Usually, a person has more faith in their fear than in their future."

—Doug Firebaugh

Foreword by Andrea Waltz & Richard Fenton, authors of *Go for No!*

THE MOST EXPENSIVE COOKIES IN THE WORLD

A RECIPE FOR PROSPECTING <u>WITHOUT</u> FEAR OF REJECTION

Russ McNeil

THE MOST EXPEN$IVE COOKIES IN THE WORLD

A Recipe for Prospecting <u>Without</u> Fear of Rejection

To order additional copies of this book, visit www.AhaUniversity.com.

Cover illus: Orara, Jose (aka, Salamander VII). 2012. www.JoseOrara.Homestead.com.

Cover design: Mayfield, Damien. 2012. www.DamienMayfield.com.

Mrs. Fields is a registered trademark of The Mrs. Fields' Brand, Inc. South Salt Lake City UT.

ISBN: 978-1-936417-99-5
Library of Congress Control Number: *TBD*
Printed in United States of America

*G*ratitudinals

Our Heavenly Father is willing to share His talents, but not His glory. In the case of this book, it's obvious that He shared His talents because it wouldn't have been possible any other way. I enthusiastically give Him all the glory for it.

A number of special people have contributed to the journey that led to this book: Larry Lenamond, David Hott, Don Wilson, Dean Lindsay and Brian Mast. Each of you contributed to the recipe inside this book. When I grow up, I want to be just like these guys, a world-class chef creating life-changing masterpieces.

A big shout-out goes to Richard Fenton & Andrea Waltz. Your expertise in overcoming rejection makes the foreword you wrote all the more meaningful. Special cookies should be served from a special platter and the foreword you wrote is something special indeed. It means more than you may know.

More sincere thanks go to several talented individuals:

- 👍 Damien Mayfield for the cover design and Jose Orara for the custom illustration on the cover (credits, facing page)

- 👍 Daniel & Denna Ferguson for proof-reading so well that everyone else will think I'm actually somewhat literate

- 👍 Brian Boyne for assuming the role of Guinea Pig in order to provide a reader's perspective of the content

I am certain that none of these hapless victims will ever eat another chocolate chip cookie for as long as they live. I can live with that. ☺

Lastly, I need to express appreciation for my one-in-a-million wife, Tammy. Your patience and discernment are God's gift to you. You are God's gift to me. It is for you that I build our businesses.

F oreword

by Richard Fenton &Andrea Waltz

Nowhere is rejection more of an issue than in the profession of network marketing. As the authors of a book that teaches people to overcome their fear of 'no', we know this all too well. We have spoken to, and met, thousands of people in the profession who continue to battle the challenge of rejection.

That's right; it's a battle. And like every great battle, there are twists and turns, ups and downs and times when hope is lost entirely. Tragically, some people succumb, and ultimately lose this battle. We use this analogy not to depress or alarm you, but to stress the utmost importance of utilizing every resource available to help you continuously and rigorously feed your brain with positive, inspiring and new ways to overcome this most insidious of all challenges.

So with the topic of this battle so near and dear to us, we were quite curious to learn of Russ McNeil's latest work, *The Most Expensive Cookies in the World*. How could he possibly use cookies to create a change in mindset about rejection? It seemed like a difficult task. And that, of course, is the brilliance.

It's the parable of a world-class restaurant where you work as a server. That's right—you work there—a creative choice made by the author to put you right in the middle of the story! What's so great about all of this is that it draws you into the story immediately. Russ's writing is down to earth and easy to read and since you're the main character—well—it makes you eager to find out what's going to happen next!

In the story, you find yourself befriending a frequent patron. At the same time, you find yourself part of the restaurant's exciting new launch of the best, most delicious, most unbelievable cookies ever baked. (Warning: while reading this: you may find yourself overtaken with an overwhelming urge to run out, grab some chocolate chip cookie dough and start baking.)

Needless to say, the analogy totally works and like the first bite of a really delicious cookie, it's even better than you expect.

As you finally reach the conclusion and with the lessons digested, we think you'll be plenty full. Perhaps not so much in your stomach (unless you did, in fact, bake cookies), but rather full of hope and of knowledge.

Truly, the lessons you'll learn in this book will help you win the most crucial battle of all—the battle over your networking marketing mindset. It's a battle that you *can* win—if you're willing to feed your brain with the good stuff. And you won't find very many things better than a story about the most delicious cookies ever made with some of the most life-altering lessons ever shared.

Go ahead—have a cookie—turn the page and dig in! We dare you to eat just one.

Richard Fenton and Andrea Waltz,

Authors of the best-selling book:

Go for No! Yes is the Destination...No is How You Get There

*D*ear Reader...

I once had the occasion to hear Debbi Fields speak at a business conference. As founder of Mrs. Fields®, she's an astute business person, and I enjoyed her speech immensely. Of all the things she shared, one thing in particular stood out...

"I've never felt like I was in the cookie business. I've always been in a feel-good business. My job is to sell joy. My job is to sell happiness. My job is to sell an experience."

What a great description—for her, and perhaps even more so for us. It feels good to use a product or service that enhances your life. It feels good to build a business that affords you the ability to make significant choices. Our profession is jam-packed full of positive experiences. And it's your job to sell those experiences.

Now don't get all wrapped around the axle because I used the "S" word (sell). Whether we admit it or not, we all are in sales. Zig Ziglar defines sales as "the transfer of belief." By that definition, anyone building an opportunity-based business is *definitely* in sales. And in our profession, the number one job is to sell experiences... life-enhancing, destiny-altering experiences.

Our business, just like Debbi's, begins with a cookie. And our cookies, just like Debbi's, are truly something special. This book is about sharing the magic of gourmet cookies. It's not so much about the cookies themselves though. No, this book is more about the process of sharing and the experiences that come with it.

That's where the *real* magic is.

Bon appétit.

Russ

P reface

When I was a kid, I used to love to go to my grandmother's house. She lived within easy driving distance, so the trip itself wasn't particularly exciting. Our excitement stemmed from something much more tasty than a car ride—her cooking—especially her desserts.

My personal favorites were her cookies; peanut butter, chocolate chip, macadamia nut or any other kind for that matter. I can still remember the aroma filling her house from end to end, the delicious scrumptious taste and the warm chewy texture to which words could never do justice.

My grandmother knew nothing about sharing a business opportunity, but, through her cookies, she sure could share an experience—my goodness, could she ever. Those are fond memories; the kind of experiences you wish you could store in a bottle and open to savor only on special occasions.

I don't know about you, but this author knows absolutely nothing about baking cookies. I have, however, learned a thing or two about sharing an opportunity, my goodness, have I ever. Prospecting was the only way to keep my business alive. My so-called warm market turned out to be rather chilly; bottom-line: none of them were interested; zip, zilch, nada, not one among them; no not one. Sound familiar?

This situation is fairly common. So what is one to do? The course of action most people take is to quit. They puff out their chest and proudly proclaim something like, "This business just isn't for me," as if the proclamation justifies their lack of determination. How 'bout that one? Does it sound familiar?

For me, quitting was never an option. I don't quit. Anything. Ever. Period. The only alternative I had was to figure out how to meet new people, people I didn't already know. In other words, I needed a recipe for prospecting strangers. It took quite a while to develop that recipe. I won't bother listing all the nauseating ingredients and spices I experimented with in the beginning, but suffice it to say that it was Nast-ee (with a capital 'N'). As distasteful as that process was, I did eventually develop a deliciously duplicable, hypo-allergenic, zero-calorie recipe for prospecting. The necessary ingredients include, among others, knowing what to say, knowing how to say it, and a structured system of productive beliefs. One thing *not* in the recipe is fear of rejection.

> "I could write an entertaining novel about rejection slips, but I fear it would be overly long."
>
> —Louise Brown

Don't be alarmed, nearly everyone has at least some fear of rejection when they first start in our profession. So if you have a fear of rejection, congratulations! You're perfectly normal, but you *don't* have to stay that way. For a wholesome prospecting recipe to work—for you to master the prospecting process— you will need to sift out the fear of rejection. And that is precisely what this book is about—empowering you to step past your fear of rejection and leaving it right where it belongs—in the past.

What Causes Fear of Rejection?

A quick on-line search will reveal a plethora of articles that address this question. One popular explanation is that fear of rejection stems from beliefs planted when we were children. Typical explanations include the frequency with which children hear the words "no" and "can't" (e.g., "No, Jonny. Don't do that, you may fall."). Now, don't get me wrong. The constant bombardment of negative messages *does* have an effect, a profoundly inhibiting effect, but the inhibiting beliefs formed from these messages do *not* cause fear of rejection.

So what *does* cause fear of rejection? The short answer is surprisingly simple, but let me warn you: it's not very appetizing. In fact, when you hear the answer, it may taste more like castor oil than cookie dough. The truth is that fear of rejection is 100% self-inflicted. We truly do bring it upon ourselves.

Have you ever heard of the "5A's"? They are a̲chievement, a̲uthority, a̲ffluence, a̲ppearance and a̲dmiration. Our society places a tremendous emphasis on the 5A's (Souba 2006), and as individuals, we crave them, we *need* them. Fear of rejection is a side-effect of the later two, appearance and admiration. "We work hard to acquire them because they make us look good, stand out and be accepted" (Souba 2006).

Appearance has to do with our perception of how others see us. We want to appear knowledgeable, not ignorant. We want others to see us as organized and "put together," not incompetent or bungling. We have a need to "look good" well beyond our superficial, external physical attributes. Now, consider this need within the context of your prospecting efforts. How would you look if the prospect asks a question for which you have no answer? Unknowledgeable? Amateurish? How would you look, if you stumble over your words? Incompetent? Inept? After all, you get nervous when you prospect. It's easy to make mistakes.

Admiration has to do with the need to be popular, accepted and well-liked. What would happen if you offered your opportunity to a prospect only to learn that the person can't stand your type of business? If he doesn't like your business, he won't like you either, right? How many times have you heard that most people just won't "get" the business? If they don't accept your business, how can they possibly accept you? Neither of these conclusions is correct. They're not even logical, but that doesn't matter because your need for admiration isn't based on logic either.

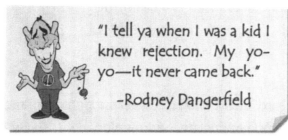

"I tell ya when I was a kid I knew rejection. My yo-yo—it never came back."

-Rodney Dangerfield

A need is anything that is essential to your survival. Clearly, you won't meet your demise merely from looking foolish to a prospect. And believe it or not, not having all the answers isn't a terminal condition either. Prospecting *is* a contact sport, but the contact is rarely fatal. Our *conscious* mind understands this, but our beliefs and needs don't reside in our conscious mind. They exist in our *sub*conscious mind, and *that*, my friend, is a completely different matter.

4

The subconscious mind is not logical; not one tiny little bit. It doesn't differentiate between fact and fiction either. You simply cannot reason with the subconscious mind. How many times have you had the opportunity to prospect a person and yet you hesitate? You mentally go through all the reasons that you should make an offer. You tell yourself "the worst that can happen is for the prospect to say 'no'". Yet, something still holds you back. Ever been there? Sure you have; we all have. There are a couple of things that can hold you back from prospecting and one of them is fear of rejection (see inset for the other).

By default, needs overshadow

> Something else that can paralyze your prospecting efforts is a category I call Inhibiting Beliefs. This includes unproductive thoughts such as *"The prospect may think I'm taking advantage them"* and *"It's self-serving to approach people I don't even know."* There are many such thoughts. They are highly toxic and, left untreated, can cause permanent paralysis. Fortunately, there is an antidote. Visit here, (www.AhaUniversity.com) or email to discover more.

desires. Our need to preserve appearance and admiration override our desire to prospect. If the act of prospecting threatens our need to look good, then we may avoid prospecting altogether. It matters not how much you try to reason with yourself. Why? Because the thing holding you back, your need to look good, resides in your subconscious mind, and you cannot reason with it. It's simply not possible.

Cheer up. There is a way to get off the yes-I-can-no-I-can't merry-go-round. Anyone can do it. It's not even difficult. You'll need a new horse to ride on, some new information, information of which you may not currently be aware, but that's easy. Keep reading. The ride is about to begin.

Why Not Call it *"Discomfort of Rejection"*?

Appearance and admiration are not luxuries; they're needs. This means they're necessary for survival. Thus, anything that prevents your needs from being met, threatens your survival.

Your subconscious mind is where these threats are perceived and it doesn't know the difference between fact and fiction. So, in a very real sense, when your need to look good or your need to be accepted is threatened, your subconscious is concerned for your very survival. Now, let me ask you, if you were being chased by a full-grown bear with a full-grown appetite, would you be in a state of fear or a state of discomfort? The answer is obvious; you would be in fear and you would do everything in your power to avoid the bear.

Threaten a need and your subconscious mind reacts the very same way, by doing everything in its power to avoid the threat. It's enough to keep some reps from prospecting at all. Good-bye, Mr. Prospect. I'd love to stay and chat, but I need to outrun Mr. Bear; he's just too scary to for me to stay around and yak about business.

So Real You Can Taste it, Touch it and Smell it

Some people think that fear of rejection is an emotion and some think of it as a simple mental attitude ("it's all in your head" if you will). No matter how you classify it, you have to agree that

6

fear of rejection is intangible. You can't touch it, you can't taste it and you can't smell it. Isn't it ironic that something so intangible can affect us in a manner is that is so very tangible?

Sometimes, the best way to solve a problem is to find a different approach; look at the issue from a different angle, through a different pair of lenses. Fear of rejection is one of those issues.

We're going to look at the subject from a whole new perspective. This new perspective will take the *in*tangible and make it entirely tangible. You will see fear of rejection through a new pair of lenses. In so doing, you will gain new insights into the issue. More importantly, you become empowered—empowered to rise above the challenge, empowered to break the grip that is strangling your prospecting efforts.

The content in this book is not an experiment, and it's not on trial either. On the contrary, this book was born out of a PowerPoint presentation I developed a few years ago. Judging from audience feedback, the presentation is right on the money. It brings clarity to the issue in a unique way. With this clarity comes a newfound confidence, a confidence so real, you can touch it, taste it, smell it. A confidence so real, you'll be able to take action. And in this case, action means prospecting—without the fear of rejection, and *that* means you'll be able to sell more experiences.

My grandmother would be proud.

P *arable Powered*

What you're about to read is an illustration. Some might call it a metaphor. I prefer the term parable, and because my name is on the cover, I get to choose, so parable it is. It's not a short parable, after all, it takes up the remainder of the book, but don't fret. It reads fast, it's got plenty of low-carb white space, and it's seasoned with a liberal scoop of cartoon morsels. And guess what? You're in it! In fact, you're the main character. *That* ought to make the time fly. If nothing else, it'll keep your attention—you never know what crazy things I may have you doing. Easy now, don't choke on your cookie; I promise to keep the pain to a minimum.

Your Life—an Alternative Version

Sometimes, I think about what my life would be like if I had made different choices along the way. What if I had not conspired with a high school friend to arrange an introduction to the gorgeous creature who became my wife? *That* would have changed some things. What if I had earned my degree in a different major? I probably would not have met David, the person who introduced me to the networking profession, and chances are the book you are reading wouldn't even exist. Wow, all these yummy cookies and no one to write the recipe— what a waste *that* would have been.

What would *your* life be like if *you* had made different choices along the way? Keep reading and find out. The story that follows is based on an alternative version of your life.

Relax. I'll leave out the embarrassing parts; you know—like the polyester leisure suit still hanging in your closet. And remember that time in Belize with the ill-mannered monkey and that crazy cross-eyed parrot? I'll definitely leave that out—heck, that story makes *me* blush and I wasn't even there! What I *will* include though, is a wee bit of poetic license. It's all part of the parable and it's all about you…

5-star (★ ★ ★ ★ ★) History Buff

For as long as you can remember, you've been fascinated with history. Your idea of a dream job is curator at the Smithsonian. That's why you worked so hard for acceptance into one of the nation's top liberal arts schools. You even received a partial scholarship. It's a good thing too because otherwise, you couldn't have afforded the tuition.

Even so, the scholarship itself is not enough to cover all of your expenses. To help offset the costs, you took a part-time job. As do many college students, you find the most viable option for part-time employment in the restaurant industry. When you're not in class or studying, you're practicing the fine art of table service. As it turns out, you're quite good at it. You're personable, attentive and polite. The restaurant patrons must appreciate you because you always seem to earn more in tips than anyone else on the staff.

After a while, you decide to take your experience and reputation to a different restaurant, one of higher quality (and

9

having a more expensive menu). You learn more about the industry and you earn significantly more too. It works out so well, that you repeat the process and apply as waiter in an even nicer restaurant and, again, your income increases.

Early in your third year of college, you upgrade one final time. By this time, you're a seasoned veteran and a top-earner in a 5-star restaurant. You even have a loyal following among the regular patrons.

Friends, Tips and Books

This loyal following among the restaurant's patrons is a source of personal pride. It's the ultimate measure of a job well-done. While you enjoy waiting on all the regulars, you naturally have your favorites. And of the select few whom you consider your personal favorites, one in particular stands out above the rest.

From the very first time you waited on the couple, it's obvious there's something special about them. The moment you approach their table, they preempt the conversation by introducing themselves to you. The genuineness of their smiles is impressive. So is the way they use words to build you up, to compliment you. And they are so sincere. You feel like the most important person in the room. Isn't that *your* job? It's as if you and they have reversed roles. How do they do that? You'll have your answer soon enough.

They frequent the restaurant a couple times a month, sometimes just the two of them, sometimes with friends, and sometimes with a *lot* of friends. However unlikely it may seem, *all* of their friends, without exception, have the same knack for making the people around them feel special. Imagine spending your life surrounded by so many quality people. How do they manage to pull *that* off?

Whenever they bring friends, the entire party seems to be in the midst of a celebration—not a birthday or anniversary—you see enough of those celebrations to spot them right away. These get-togethers are something else entirely. It seems almost as if they're gathered to celebrate a job promotion. That explanation doesn't really fit either though because you hear enough of their conversations to know that they're all self-employed. Perhaps the celebrations have more to do with business accomplishments. Whatever it is, they're all glad to be a part of it.

Whatever the occasion and whatever the party size, you're all too glad that they request you as their server—man do these people tip. Words are one thing, but their tips—well, when it comes to expressing appreciation, they really put their money where their mouth is.

And then there are the books. In addition to generous cash tips, the couple also gives books, actual hardcopy books. The first time you wait on them, they give you a paperback titled *How to Win Friends and Influence People* by Dale something-or-a-another. Naturally, you thank them, but still, it catches you off guard and you aren't entirely sure how to respond.

> "Miss a meal if you have to, but don't miss a book."
>
> –Jim Rohn

With your studies you don't have much free time to read, but you know one thing with absolute certainty: you're not about to offend your favorite patrons, and biggest tippers, by setting the book aside without reading at least part of it. Surprisingly, you actually enjoy the book. It's loaded with a powerful mix of wisdom and common sense. Oddly enough, even though you've never read it before, the material seems vaguely familiar. Nevertheless, you definitely see how the information applies to your job, and you're grateful for the gift.

During their next visit, the couple mentions how they see you employing ideas from the book. It feels good to have them notice. You don't know it yet, but it's a test; did you, or did you not take the book seriously? In the future, you will learn that reading and applying the lessons in that book proves to be a pivotal point in your story, a life-changing choice. As a reward for passing the undisclosed test, the couple gifts you a second book, *The Go-Giver*.

> "Outside of a dog, a book is man's best friend. Inside of a dog, it's too dark to read."
>
> –Groucho Marx

This new book is a fast read with an insightful message and it has an immediate effect on your thought process. Your outlook toward other people changes forever. Your favorite patrons see, and comment on, these effects during their next visit. You've noticed the changes too, and you like what you see. And just like that, you're hooked—you need more—more positive change, more of the same kind of information, more, more, more.

Over the next few months, this cycle of gift/read/test repeats a number of times, all without your knowledge. They gift you copies of some great books: *Positive Personality Profiles*, *The Greatest Salesman in the World*, *The Ultimate Gift* and *Rhinoceros*

"A person who is nice to you, but rude to the waiter, is *not* a nice person."

–Dave Barry

Success. By reading them and applying what you learn, you demonstrate a choice few people ever make—the choice of making a genuine commitment to personal development. And just like that, the tests cease, but you don't realize it because the gift books keep coming.

My Patron, My Sponsor

The couple's next visit will prove to be another watershed moment in your life. As they prepare to leave, they share how pleased they are to see your recent personal development. You can hardly take the credit. They're the ones who whetted your appetite for this new brand of information. You owe them a debt of gratitude and you tell them so. Then, for the first time, he makes a direct reference to their business. That's the moment you learn that it's possible build a business by taking an interest in people and helping them to reach their full potential.

Needless to say, *that* idea raises a few questions. The couple recognizes the curious look on your face, but you have other tables requiring your attention. In parting, he asks if you want to know more. Of course you do. So, you trade phone numbers and he leaves you with some simple instructions:

"That number I gave you is to a pre-recorded six-minute overview. I'll call you on Thursday afternoon to see if there's any common interest. If you like what you hear, we can visit over half a cup of coffee and fill in the gaps. If not, no harm done. Does that sound fair?"

Is he kidding? Did he really ask, "If it sounds fair?" Of course, it's fair. It's more than fair! Your mind is already racing with the possibilities and you still have absolutely no information to go on.

The next day, you call and listen to the recording. It doesn't answer all your questions. In fact, it actually raises a few new ones, but still, something is drawing you toward the concept. Could it be that your interest has more to do with the people than it does the recording?

Your imagination is still in overdrive when the phone rings on Thursday afternoon. The conversation is short—yes, you listened to the recording, yes, you would like to know more, and yes, you have some time Friday afternoon for a short visit at the local coffee shop.

To call Friday's chat enlightening, is a massive understatement. You're there for only forty-four minutes, but in that time, you learn the answers to nearly every one of your questions. You see an overview of the products and the benefits they offer and you see an overview of the compensation plan, but these overviews are *not* what you *learn*.

What you *learn*, is why the concepts in *How to Win Friends and Influence People* seemed so familiar even as you were reading them for the first time—because your patron couple has been practicing the concepts from the first moment you met them. You *learn* that by relating to people where they are, you open the door for positive influence. You *learn* that through effective communication, you can encourage the people around you to share a common vision. You *learn* that by employing all these consistently and sincerely, you inevitably surround yourself with people empowered to attain their full potential; you end up surrounded by an army of quality friends.

You are astounded at the implications of the business opportunity before you. During that momentous chat, you hear one statement, in particular, that stands out. You'll never forget it:

> "When I first started this profession, I thought 'What a great business—a fabulous compensation plan, plus I get to learn how to be a better person.' After a while, I realized my mistake. The truth is that I had it backward. What we really have is a personal development program with a compensation plan attached."

He finished the visit by inviting you to join his team. And that's how your favorite patron became your sponsor.

The next day, your sponsor sits down with you and gets you started properly. He helps you to document your goals, set up a game-plan, introduces you to other members of the team and conducts a great little tutorial on how and why to use third-party tools (like the recording you listened to, DVD's, and magazines).

He also tells you something very interesting. He explains that the gift books are one of the ways he "gives back" and he routinely hands them out as a tokens of appreciation. He continues by explaining that you represent a unique situation. Typically, he never knows whether a person reads the gift or not, but, because he and his spouse see you regularly during their restaurant visits, they have the unique, and rewarding, opportunity to observe someone accept the gifts and actually put them to use. Then he points out that they had not planned to approach you with their business. Only after an extended period of watching you grow through personal development did they decide to do so. He finished by saying,

"This will mean more as you learn more, but for now just realize that the way this conversation came about is very unusual. You will not be handing out gift books to sponsor people."

On the way back to your dorm, you marvel at what had just transpired. What if you had chosen to not read that first book? And then it hits you—a profound realization—that the choices people make, even the seemingly insignificant ones, sometimes have within them, the capacity to change destinies.

> "Most homes valued at over $1,000,000 have a library. That should tell us something."
> –Jim Rohn

Not Just Another Cookie

On the following week, the owner of the restaurant makes an exciting announcement. A pastry chef of international renown has agreed to join the restaurant's roster of premier chefs.

Pastry chefs are responsible for desserts and baked goods. This particular chef specializes in the latter. And of all the delectable delicacies for which he is so renowned, none are more loved than his cookies. And of all the cookie recipes he has to his credit, none are more celebrated than his one-of-a-kind recipe for chocolate chip cookies.

The chef requires you to sample his specialties prior to serving them. You have no choice but to dive in, so that's exactly what you do. Without wasting any time, you quickly rescue the nearest chocolate chip cookie from the lustful stares of your co-workers. With a triumphant snicker, and a mischievous expression, you take your first bite. Instantly, you sense that your taste buds may never be the same.

Now, you can buy chocolate chip cookies in a bag and you can bake them on your own, but what you *can't* do is duplicate this particular recipe. This pastry chef didn't build his reputation on mundane run-of-the-mill recipes.

He calls them chocolate chip cookies, but that name is woefully inadequate. For starters, these chocolate chip cookies are enormous, having the diameter of miniature Frisbees. They're packed with chips all right, but don't think for a minute that *all* the chips are chocolate. Some are semi-sweet butterscotch chips, also made from scratch.

The texture of these mega-caloric creations is sublime. The contrast between the hard, crunchy crust and the soft, chewy inside defies words. And when you raise one of these delectable discs to take a bite, prepare yourself. Just about the time you open your mouth, a warm wave of aromatic delight washes over and envelops your entire sense of smell.

Somewhere between the second and third bite, you recognize the taste of cinnamon; not much; just a touch; just the perfect amount to compliment the cornucopia of other flavors. After another bite or two, you recognize the unmistakable hint of peanut butter. How does he manage to use just the right amount? To call your encounter with these extraordinary cookies a religious experience might be an exaggeration, but not much of one.

About half way through the decadent dessert, you notice it for the first time. Well, at least you *think* you notice it. You're not sure what it is, and you're not sure which sense picked it up first, smell or taste. In fact, you're not certain it's even really there at all. After a couple more bites, and after careful consideration of the Tango of tastes dancing in your mouth, you decide that it is indeed real, not your imagination. And then, with the next bite, your doubts return. What *is* that flavor? Don't bother asking the chef. His only response is a wry smile and a twinkle in his eye.

Sometimes the Best Things Really *are* Free

The restaurant owner is elated about having the new chef onboard. After sampling his recipes, you understand why. Surely once word gets out, the restaurant will be standing room only every night, not just on weekends.

The owner realizes that the best way to get the word out is to elicit the help of existing patrons. After all, the most effective advertising is word-of-mouth. The best way to elicit their help is to give them something new and exciting to talk about. So, the owner devises a plan.

The plan is simple. Each night, the chef conjures up a different one of his world-famous specialties for promotional purposes and each night the wait staff offers *complimentary* servings of that night's specialty as part of their dessert presentations. The owner hopes, that by offering the culinary concoctions on a complimentary basis, patrons are more willing to try items that, otherwise, they might never order. If only a few patrons spread the word about the superlative specialties, the results will make the plan worthwhile.

It's a fool-proof plan. No one can mess this up. Not even the worst waiter you've ever worked with. Not even a certain ill-mannered monkey.

Simply Irresistible

The big night arrives. Tonight you will give away platter after platter of world-class desserts for free. When you clock in, you're thrilled to learn that the dessert of the night is none other than the world-famous, life-altering chocolate chip cookies. You joke that you hope the chef has his baker's hat on, because you'll have every one of those cookies handed out just about as fast as he can yank 'em out of the oven.

Who in their right mind would pass up one of *these* chocolate chip cookies, especially if they're free? Not any of the patrons you wait on, that's for sure.

How could anyone turn down these colossal creations—the culinary combination of hot, sticky, semi-melted texture and the multitudinous yummy, sweet tastes? How indeed? You can't help but recall the other night when you ate one for the first time. There's so much more to these cookies than what meets the eye. You wonder why the other desserts are even on the menu. Truly, they are what every patron wants in a dessert. Even the patrons with no sweet tooth will gobble these fast enough to turn Cookie Monster green with envy. You have no doubt that the patrons will be eating eat right out of your hands. (Make sure you wash 'em.)

Was it something you said?

The restaurant begins to fill up quickly; looks like it's going to be a busy night; all the more people with which to share the complimentary desserts. Your anticipation for the night builds even more when you see your sponsors, that cherished couple, sitting at their favorite table.

Your initial assessment proves correct—the night is busy and hectic. Eventually, the first round of meals winds down and you're delighted to see that your sponsors are the first ones ready for dessert. You're all too eager to accommodate them.

As you approach their table carrying the very first platter of those uncanny cookies, those miraculous munchies, you can't help the impish grin on your face, the conspiratorial look in your eye. When it comes to these cookies, you never forget your first. Thus, with keen expectation, you anticipate celebrating their delight as they too revel in their own encounter with the captivating combination of calico flavors.

You present the platter with flair and recite a glowing review of the indescribable experience which awaits them. Then without further ado, you select a pair of the divine delicacies and prepare to set them before your precious sponsors, and at that very same moment, they both, in unison, politely...decline.

What?! How could they possibly pass? Were they not listening to the details in your description? What part of tantalizing texture and succulent sweetness did they not understand? Are you not their favorite waiter? Are you not an adopted member of their business family? How could they tell *you* "no?" In short, you're flabbergasted and your fizzling facial expression screams so, loud and clear.

A Different Kind of Fortune Cookie

Your sponsor notices the unmistakable expression of baffled befuddlement. He responds with a very different expression of his own—one of benign bemusement—as if he sees an unexpected opportunity to impart some particularly valuable wisdom. And indeed, he does.

You're on the clock and surrounded by occupied tables, hardly the time and place to attend a seminar. Nevertheless, your sponsor is never one to pass on the chance to turn an everyday experience into a priceless lesson. With this in mind, he decides that, in place of ordering dessert, to initiate a brief conversation...

S: "You look disappointed that we passed on the cookies."

Y: "I am disappointed—and surprised. They're very good."

S: "Did you expect everyone in here to eat one?"

Y: "Of course, they're amazing cookies."

S: "You know, those cookies you're holding, are worth a fortune."

Y: "How's that?"

S: "Well it's a two-step process. We don't have time to get into it right now, but you can get started tonight."

Y: "What do I need to do?"

S: "Make a note of all the different responses you get as you go around handing out those cookies."

Y: "And then what?"

S: "And then we go through step 2 together. We sit down for a few minutes when you're not on the clock, and go through the list."

Chocolate Chips to Fortune ¢ookie$

His proposal seems vague, a bit mysterious even. You, of all people, appreciate the richness of the chocolate chip cookies, but what part do they play in your personal wealth? If the previous training session with your sponsor is any indication, you're confident that you'll soon find out.

In keeping with the restaurant owner's new marketing plan, you bring the complimentary specialties to each and every table as part of the expected dessert presentations. To deliver those divinely delicious delicacies, you parade across the floor with the pageantry so befitting the blue-ribbon masterpieces.

> "Help! I'm being held prisoner in a Chinese bakery!"
>
> *- Disturbing fortune cookie*

As you make your way past less fortunate tables, still awaiting their turn, a lip-smacking aroma wafts in your wake.

As the night progresses, you do indeed hand out quite a few of the cookies, more than the rest of the staff. Still, it bothers you how many patrons decline your cookie offer. The restaurant staff is a team and you take your position on that team seriously. So you can't help but wonder: is there something you can say or do to elicit more interest? After all, you know how fantastic the cookies are and you believe it's an experience everyone else will enjoy as well.

Despite the sporadic negative responses, you're still curious as to what the chocolate chip cookies have to do with your personal fortune. That's why you carefully record a list of the different patron responses. In a couple of days, you hope to find out why the list is so important.

> Up to this point, our story has been developing background, framing the context, setting the stage. The section that follows is the completion of the story. It exposes the lessons of the cookies (which is, after all, the purpose of the book). I chose to reveal all of the lessons within a single conversation. This allows the explanations to fit naturally into the parable and to flow in a conversational manner. The subheadings are a convenience to help you to refer back to specific objections, but keep in mind that the dialogue represents a single conversation. Read it as such.

Well, it's about Time

In fact, you're *so* curious about the lesson at hand that you arrive fifteen minutes earlier than the agreed upon time. Your sponsor, as usual, walks in perfectly on time, not one minute early and not one minute late. And he's not even wearing a watch. You jokingly ask if he's OCD about time and, after laughing along with you, he explains that punctuality is a matter of honoring your word and respecting the other person's time; funny how he manages to turn your fleeting comment into another worthwhile lesson. You can hardly wait to see what he does with your soon-to-be famous "Cookie Excuse List."

My Sponsor, My Mentor

"You know, I really did want one of those cookies you were handing out the other night."

"You did? Then why did you pass?" you say with a surprised tone in your voice.

"To test your reaction," he grins knowingly.

"In other words, you planned to use the cookies as a lesson."

"Well, 'planned' might be overstating it, but I did see a potential opportunity to use the cookies as an illustration. You brought your list of the different patron responses, right?"

"Yes," you confirm; your voice full of anticipation.

"Then apparently, the idea has *some* merit."

Thus begins another paradigm-changing conversation with your sponsor. This time, you recognize that fact ahead of time and you tell him so.

"I'll always be your sponsor, but, as of this conversation, our relationship enters a new phase. As of right now, I consider myself more of a mentor."

And just like that, a shift occurs and the lesson begins.

"When I mentor a person, I like to use everyday situations as illustrations. Your experience the other night, handing out the complimentary desserts, makes a great illustration for today's lesson. This lesson even comes with a title: 'The Most Expensive Cookies in the World'.

"Think about your business for a moment. When you identify someone to offer your product to, that person is a prospective customer. When you identify someone to offer your opportunity to, that person is a prospective business partner. Let's call both these groups *prospects*."

"Okay, I'm with you."

"The patrons in the restaurant the other night are like your business prospects. You offered them cookies, but you didn't know ahead of time which ones would be interested. Am I right?"

"Yes. When my shift started, I assumed that they would *all* be interested, but man was *that* a mistake," you say, still wondering what had gone wrong.

"But the point is: it was your job to offer the cookies to all of them and you didn't know ahead of time which ones would be interested."

"That's right."

"Okay. Now imagine that those same chocolate chip cookies are, in fact, DVD's or other prospecting tools. You follow?"

"I think so. If I understand correctly, you're saying that offering the cookies to my restaurant patrons is the same as offering DVD's to my business prospects."

"Yes, DVD's or magazines, or sizzle calls or any other appropriate prospecting tool. You may not have realized it until just now, but the other night you were prospecting your patrons. My definition of prospecting is this: the process of using effective communication to meet people, uncover their needs and *potentially* offer a solution.

"Am I making sense so far?"

You assure him that he is making perfect sense.

"Great. Here's where the illustration gets even better: the responses you heard from your patrons are the same kinds of things you'll hear from your prospects."

"So *that's* why you wanted me to bring the list of the different things my patrons said as I offered them cookies."

"Precisely. We're going to discuss each response in detail, but before we get into the specifics, let's go over some of the more general aspects of prospecting."

"I'm ready," you reply eagerly as you pick up your pen.

"Then let's dive in. Prospecting is like a four-legged stool—remove one of the legs and it just doesn't work as well. You can still sit on it, but it takes extra effort to keep it upright. The four legs of prospecting are COMMUNICATION, PROJECTION, CONTEMPLATION and FORTIFICATION. I'll explain a little about each one and then we'll discuss how the various patron responses fit in.

"As we go through these, there's no need to feel overwhelmed. It may sound like a lot, but it really isn't. Ninety percent of prospecting is having the right information. And even though we won't cover it all today, I will point out some great resources that will help you to master this crucial skill.

"COMMUNICATION has to do with how you communicate with prospects. This includes what things to say, how to say them and when to say them. Communication isn't limited to verbal communication either. It also includes non-verbal communication, things like body-language and behavioral styles. As your mentor, I recommend you get your hands on a book titled *Prospecting Rules*. It's a fast read that covers the subject of prospecting communication in a humorous and concise way like none other.

"The second leg of prospecting is PROJECTION. This has to do with the image you project to the prospect before, during and after a prospecting encounter. For example, appearing relaxed even though you feel nervous is something you can project. Coming across as reliable and trustworthy is another. There are a number of these that will make a dramatic difference in your results. Many are common sense once they're explained, but it's hard to find solid information on the subject. Nearly everything I know about this leg of prospecting, I learned from a book titled, *Lessons from the Ark*. This is one of the most unique little books you'll ever read and it is spot on. I've never met the author, but clearly, with respect to prospecting, he's been there and done that. This book is a perfect complement to the other one I mentioned.

"Any questions so far?"

"No sir, I'm right there with you."

"Good. The third leg of prospecting is CONTEMPLATION. Contemplation refers to the things that go through your mind whenever you think about prospecting. The things that go through your mind are determined by your innermost beliefs. Your actions will always follow these beliefs. For example, if you believe that it is self-serving to prospect people you don't know, then your prospecting efforts are severely hampered. Similarly, if you have concerns that prospects see you as taking advantage of them, then some of your inner beliefs are seriously out-of-whack which in turn, makes you much less effective. Inhibiting beliefs are the single biggest *de*tractor from your prospecting efforts. This is a complete subject all by itself

27

and we won't broach it today. I recommend that you look into an audio program titled _Sticks and Stones._ This program includes both a humorous overview of how beliefs affect your prospecting *plus* a tool designed to eradicate any inhibiting beliefs that may be holding you back.

"The fourth, and final, leg of the prospecting stool is FORTIFICATION. This leg has to do with preparing yourself to withstand attacks from the fear of rejection. Everyone has a different level of tolerance for rejection. People who are new to the networking profession are particularly susceptible to the effects of this 'silent killer'. This is the subject we'll focus on today. By the time you and I go through your list of patron responses you'll have your own 5-star recipe—a recipe for crumbling the fear of rejection.

"Let's recap real quick. There are four legs to prospecting. You know about some resources that will help with the first three and we'll address the fourth one by going through your list. Are we on the same page of the cookbook?"

"Absolutely."

What else could you say? Your mentor has a gift for making everything seem so clear.

"Excellent. Let's get to that list you made. Here's what we're going to do: you read off a response, and we'll discuss it from two perspectives. The first perspective will be that of your restaurant patron. For the other perspective we'll explore the similarities between what your patron said as you offered a cookie and what you may hear a prospect say as you offer a prospecting tool."

"Similarities? Do prospects really say the same things that my patrons said," you ask skeptically.

"Not word-for-word mind you, but the parallels may surprise you. What's first on your list?"

1. No thanks. I couldn't eat another bite!

"I heard this response from several patrons," you offer as an opening comment.

"And what was your reaction?"

"I thought, 'You've got to be kidding me! If you had any idea how good these things are you would've asked for them before the main course.' Naturally, I didn't actually *say* that..."

"So let me make sure I understand. You're saying that the cookies are so special that you believe the patrons would prefer to fill up on *them* rather than say...a steak or lobster?"

"I know I would," you slur, struggling to contain the drool.

"I get that, but this isn't about you. It's about the patron. Look closely at his words. Put yourself in his shoes. When someone says, 'I can't eat another bite', what do they mean?"

"I suppose they mean that they are already full."

"That's exactly what they mean. The patron is simply too full to eat anything else. Some of your prospects will give you the same response. The words will be a little different. They'll probably say something like, 'I'm too busy to look at anything else,' or 'I don't have the time to do anything else', but the message is the same.

He continues with, "There are several reasons that prospects say they're too busy. Perhaps the prospect really *is* busy. I mean, who isn't these days? Keep in mind that *you* know what the DVD represents—freedom, lifestyle and peace of mind. But, the prospect has no idea what the disc represents. In short, you have a huge information advantage over the prospect. Your prospect makes a decision—in this case to not accept the disc—without having all the facts. Just like your patrons the other night. They made decisions to pass on the cookies without having any idea how great the cookies really are. Does this analogy make sense?"

"It makes perfect sense," you say, as you finish capturing the point in your notes.

"Good. This is an important lesson because it's crucial for you to understand that you will *always* know more than the prospects—you know what you're offering—they don't.

"So the number one reason prospects say they're too busy is that they don't know that the information on the DVD can relieve their busyness, not add to it. They don't realize that you're offering to be part of the solution, not part of the problem. Any questions?"

Boy, do you ever. "How do I make them understand enough to take the DVD?"

"You don't! Prospecting is *never* about conveying knowledge or sharing details. It's about sorting. You sort prospects into two groups: the ones who want to look at the information you offer, and the ones who do not."

"Okay, so how do I make them *want* to look at the information," you ask, almost desperately.

He Chuckles.

"That, my star student, is the million-dollar question and it's not really the focus of our conversation today. But, the short answer is that you don't—the prospects will sort themselves. The better you communicate and the better you project, the more your prospects will sort themselves into the 'yes' group. Read the two books I mentioned and you'll understand what I mean and how simple it is to do.

"A second reason prospects say, 'I'm too busy' is because they perceive what you are doing as too much work. Who wants to take on more work, more drudgery, more responsibility? When you have fun and demonstrate a positive demeanor, you attract people to yourself and to your offer. How many sweet cookies would you give away with a sour expression of your face?"

"Probably zero," a glimmer of understanding in your voice.

"That's an extreme example, but a realistic one. It is *you* who sets the tone of the prospecting encounter. If it looks as if you're using a lot of energy to prospect, or if you make it look like a chore, that's how the prospect perceives it. Thus, the 'I don't have time' response.

"The bottom-line is that, while you have plenty of influence over the prospecting encounter, the prospect's response is ultimately up to the prospect. And even when the response is 'I'm too busy,' the prospect is not rejecting *you*. The prospect, for whatever reason, is merely rejecting the idea of additional work. Now tell me how all this relates to fear of rejection."

"Well," you say, "if the prospect isn't rejecting me, then there is no rejection *to* fear."

"You got it! There is no fear of rejection, because there is no rejection. You should write that down. It's a powerful point.

"What's next on that list of yours?"

2. I'll wait and have one later, with my coffee.

"I heard this excuse several times also."

"Excuse? Why do you call it an excuse?"

"What else *could* it be?" you ask, as if the answer is obvious.

"Good question. Let me ask you another one. Did you offer the cookies again later when you brought out the coffee?"

"Of course, it's a 5-star restaurant. It's my job to be accommodating."

"And did these same patrons take a cookie along with their coffee?"

"Some did and some didn't."

"Okay, so back to your comment about 'excuses'. Here's what happened: some of the patrons gave you an excuse and some did not. These are two very different groups of patrons.

He goes on to explain, "The patrons who told you 'maybe later' and then later declined again for the second time, were indeed making excuses. They could see how delicious the cookies look and they couldn't help but notice the delicious aroma too. Trust me, they wanted a cookie but something held them back. It was a tough decision for these folks. They avoided making a decision by saying 'maybe' and putting you off until a later point in time. Some of your prospects will do exactly the same thing."

"How so?"

"Prospects are just like restaurant patrons—some of them have trouble making decisions—especially on-the-spot decisions. If you catch a prospect off-guard with your offer of opportunity, it can cause confusion and a confused mind does nothing. Thus, the prospect says something like, 'maybe some other time'. So, sometimes, when you hear 'maybe later', it's nothing more than a stall tactic on the part of the prospect. Does that make sense?"

"Yes. What can I do to prevent this excuse?"

"You can't prevent it completely, but you can minimize it. The more effective you are at communicating with prospects, the less likely your offer will confuse them or catch them off-guard. With a little more knowledge and some practice, you'll see what I mean."

"Okay."

"Then there's the other group of patrons, the ones who *did* take a cookie later on with their coffee. These patrons weren't making excuses. They told you 'later' and then later made good on their word, right?"

"I suppose, but why did they put it off at all? If they knew they wanted a cookie, why didn't they take one the first time I offered?"

"You tell me. Think back to these same patrons. Were they in the middle of a conversation? Engrossed in some sort of reading material? Talking on the phone?"

You unconsciously roll your eyes up and to your left. You don't even realize you're doing it, but your mentor notices. He understands that you're exercising your visual recall. More specifically, you're creating a picture in your mind of the patrons in question.

After a few brief moments, you respond with "I can't remember all of them, but now that you mention it, yes, some of them were busy doing other things."

"So, you see, these patrons weren't making excuses at all. The first time you asked, they were busy. By the time you returned and offered a cookie the second time, they were all too glad to accept."

He continues with, "Now let me ask you this: how much did you truly know about the patrons' other activities? Did you participate in their conversations? Were you tapping their phones? Looking over shoulders to read along with them?"

"Of course not."

"Of course you didn't. You run into the same exact situation when you prospect. When you step into someone's life and offer your opportunity, you have no clue what is going on in his or her life. Did he just take a new job, or was he just laid off? Did she just get married or purchase a new home? Is the prospect focused on a pressing deadline at work? What about divorce or child birth? Any number of things may be consuming the prospect's attention. Some of them are positive and some are negative, but either way, it's extremely difficult for your offer to compete with these things. Make sense?"

"I think so."

"It all comes down to timing. Is the prospect at a point in life to explore an outside opportunity? When the prospect is currently consumed with some other issue, be it positive or negative, the timing is *not* in your favor. So when prospects tell you 'maybe at a later time', they not be saying 'no', but rather, 'not at the present time'. Some will even invite you to check back in the future—with their coffee so to speak."

"So, in essence, it's out of my control?"

"Yes and no. The timing is completely out of your control, but whether you return later is very much under your control."

"How so?"

"When a prospect tells you 'maybe later' ask for permission to keep them informed."

"How do I do that?"

"Just ask. Like this: 'Do I have permission to keep you informed by checking back some other time?'"

"What if they say 'no'?" you wonder.

"If they say 'no', they were never serious about you checking back in the first place. You will find, however, that most prospects will give you permission with no hesitation."

"Really?" you ask with a note of skepticism.

"Sure they will. It's exceedingly difficult for someone to say 'no' when you're asking for permission."

"Okay. So let's say I ask for permission to keep a prospect informed and he agrees. Then what?"

"Put him on a separate list. This is a list of the prospects that tell you 'some other time' *and* give you permission to check back. We can cover the details about that in another conversation when we discuss the subject of follow-up. Right now I want to stay focused on the subject at hand—fear of rejection."

"Okay."

"So think about the two scenarios of the 'maybe later' patrons—the ones who accept your offer later and the ones who do not. Which ones rejected *you* and which ones rejected your *offer*?"

"Neither one rejected me."

"Why not?" he asks, leading you to a conclusion.

"Because even the ones who declined at a later time were merely rejecting my offer; they never rejected me personally."

"So where does that leave the fear of rejection?"

"Since there is no rejection, there is no fear of rejection" you reply.

"That's right," he affirms. "No rejection means no fear of rejection."

He continues with, "Let's summarize the 'maybe later' response. Some prospects will tell you 'maybe later'. Of those, some are merely stalling in order to avoid making a decision and some have enough interest to examine your offer at a later time. You can differentiate between the two by asking permission to keep them informed."

"Got it," you state confidently as you capture his words in your notes.

"Quit throwing softballs," he teases. Reach into that list of yours and pull out something tougher.

"Okay, you asked for it. How about this one..."

3. The last time I ate a chocolate chip cookie it made me ill.

"Heh, heh. How many times did you hear *that* one?"

"Just once, but that was enough."

"How did you respond?" he asks with a smirk of mischievousness and a large dose of curiosity.

"Not with my normal witty sense of humor, that's for sure. And the guy who said it was serious so I couldn't very well laugh. I was at a complete loss for words, which doesn't happen often."

In the spirit of fun, you decide to test your mentor with a challenge. "I bet you can't explain how a prospect might say *that*."

"Au contraire, my presumptuous pupil of prospecting, indeed, I *can* explain it. I've had prospects tell me that very same thing. Not in a long time mind you, but I've definitely heard it before."

"I can't wait to hear this..."

"You say the patron was serious about getting ill from a chocolate chip cookie?"

"Totally serious."

"Getting sick from food is no laughing matter. It's a memory that can stick with you for a long time. Sometimes the mere smell of the same food can trigger an unpleasant memory. Sometimes, this memory alone can be enough to keep you from eating that same food ever again. Has that ever happened to you?"

"Sure, it has. I bit into a rotten pecan when I was a child. Talk about nasty! To this day, I avoid pecans altogether. But what does that have to do with my prospects?"

"Your prospects have memories too. And some of their memories relate to experiences with other businesses like ours.

Then he explains further. "Our profession is only as good as the people involved and, as you know, people are all different. Some are reliable and some are irresponsible. Some are generous and some are selfish. Some are honest and some are, well, not so honest. Unfortunately, it's not always obvious who's who when you first meet them. Are you with me so far?"

"Yes."

"This means that it's possible to end up sponsored into a less-than-ideal group of individuals. Or, maybe the team is great, but the company is run by folks who may not have the best of intentions. These situations are *not* the norm. In fact, they're not even common, but they do exist. Still with me?"

"Yes, sir. One-hundred percent."

"It's possible that your prospect had an experience with the 'dark side' of some other company. He or she may have been misled or dealt with in some unfair manner. It's also possible, perhaps even likely, that the offense exists only in the mind of the prospect. Misunderstandings can occur over the slightest issues and human nature being what it is, people sometimes tell themselves pretty wild stories about being wronged, whether real or imagined.

"Nevertheless," he continues, "if a prospect perceives that he was wronged in some way, then that is his reality. When presented with another business opportunity, the prospect may very well view it through jaded glasses; he may mistakenly paint your offer with the same brush as his previous experience. Do you get the point I'm making?"

"Yes, I do. If the prospect feels like he was taken advantage of before, he may think that I represent a similar negative experience."

"Precisely. And it doesn't even matter if the offense was real, imagined, or a simple misunderstanding.

"It wasn't *your* chocolate chips cookies that made your patron ill. The quality of your cookies makes no difference. Your cookies come from a completely different recipe, but the patron's past negative experience was so overwhelming, he isn't willing to accept your offer. *You* know the quality of the cookies, *he* does not."

With this last comment, you start to connect the dots. "It's like you said earlier: I know more than the patron just like I will always know more than prospect."

"Yes! You're beginning to recognize the pattern. Now back to fear of rejection. How does it relate to the 'last one made me ill' response?"

Your mentor waits patiently while you take a moment to ponder.

"Well...the prospect is really rejecting his past experience. He's not rejecting me. He's not even rejecting my specific opportunity! He's completely off-base. That's his problem, not mine! No reason to fear that."

"That's right. Now be warned: you may feel the need to defend your opportunity or your company, to convince him of his error. Don't bother. Remember: amateurs convince, professionals sort. Any questions?"

"So there's no way to salvage the conversation?"

"Salvage? What's to salvage? You make it sound as if you're going out of your way to intentionally wreck the conversation. When you prospect properly, you create a positive experience for the prospect even when you don't get the outcome you're hoping for. Be positive and complimentary and when the prospect declines, be gracious. That way there is nothing to salvage.

Now it's your turn to put on a mischievous grin. And as you do so, you scan your list and say, "That wasn't bad. Ready for a fast ball?"

4. I can't afford to get caught cheating on my diet.

"Is that all you got?" he says, following your lead in the good-natured banter.

"You make it sound like you already have an answer," a taunting tone in your voice.

"I better have an answer for it; I had a prospect tell me the same thing a couple of week ago."

Talk about unexpected! To say your curiosity is piqued, is a massive understatement. Looks like your mentor has a fast ball of his own. Forget the contest, you're ready to dig in and learn more.

"I don't see the connection between prospecting and getting caught cheating on a diet'?"

"You will. That's why we're here. What do you think your patron meant by the 'better not get caught' comment?"

"I'm not sure. I mean obviously, I know what a diet is, but the comment about 'better not get caught' sounds ominous. I don't know what to make of that."

"Okay let's figure it out. Who do you think would be most concerned about a patron cheating on a diet?"

"Their spouse?"

"Ding! Ding! Ding! We have a winner! You are correct. And I bet every prospect who told you that they better not get caught was male. Am I correct?"

"Well, only one patron gave the response, but yes, that patron was a man. How did you know?" you ask naively.

"Go get married. Then ask me again."

"I'll take your word for it, but how does that relate to prospecting?"

"Bear with me a couple of minutes and I'll explain.

"In a typical prospecting encounter, the prospect will be alone, meaning that if prospect is married, the spouse will not be present. When you first meet a person in the absence of their significant other, you have no idea about the dynamics in their relationship. With me so far?"

"Sure."

"What you need to realize is that while the prospect may be really interested in your offer, he or she may have concerns about how the spouse will react. The spouse may be extremely receptive to an unexpected offer from a complete stranger. Then again, the spouse may not. In fact, the spouse may actually resent the fact that the prospect would even consider your offer without asking for prior approval.

"Don't get the wrong impression. Not many prospects will decline because they're worried about Wrath of Spousal Unit. Nevertheless, it is a real-world response and you should be able to recognize and understand it."

"Okay. If I understand correctly, this response is the result of the prospect keeping peace with the spouse. It has nothing to do with rejecting me."

"That's right. In fact, the prospect might be extremely interested in your offer, but if the relationship dynamics are working against you, your offer doesn't stand much of a chance."

Shaking your head in disbelief, you reply with, "It just seems so ironic. If the prospect is interested, it's probably because he wants to improve his family's lifestyle, and yet one of the very people who stands to benefit, puts the brakes on. Why is that?"

"You're absolutely right and I have no idea why. It's like Jim Rohn said, 'Don't sign up for that class.'"

"Jim Rohn?"

"Yes, R-O-H-N. He's one of my favorite teachers. Get your hands on some of his recordings. One listen and you'll know why I quote him so much.

42

Rolling right along, he says, "Here's a principle that you should write down: 'the fear of loss is always greater than the desire for gain'. The fear of loss resulting from going against the spouse completely overshadows the potential gain of pursuing an opportunity. Take a moment to digest *that*."

"I get the concept, but what do you mean by 'loss'? What does the prospect stand to actually lose?"

His eyes smile ever so subtly then he says, "Get married and ask me again."

After a moment, realization strikes and you're relieved when he rescues you from embarrassment by pressing on.

"Any more questions about the 'better not get caught' response?"

"No sir. I think I already know more about it than I care to. Is it okay if we move on to the next one?"

5. Do you think I could have a copy of the recipe?

"The other night wasn't the first time I've been asked this."

"This is a good one. "

By now, you have no doubt about it, so you say, "I'm sure it is," and, with sincere anticipation, you wait for him to continue.

"Patrons who ask this are the ones who tend to be extremely detailed and over-analytical. These are the kind of folks who proof-read photocopies. They have no intention of actually baking the cookies. They simply want to know what ingredients go into the cookies. They're curious—*very* curious.

"Some people are just inquisitive by nature. They have a need to understand, to investigate and to interrogate just about every new thing they encounter. You'll meet plenty of prospects that fit this description. Don't get me wrong, healthy curiosity is a good thing but sometimes the curiosity can get out of control. I jokingly refer to this condition as 'pathological curiosity'. One of the things I have learned is that extremely curious people also tend to be cautious. This is a generalization, of course, but it's true more often than not."

He pauses briefly and you take the opportunity to squeeze in a question. "What about me? I was curious about your business—I could hardly wait to hear you explain it."

"Yes, but you were curious because you had a genuine interest. Not all prospects that seem curious are truly interested in exploring an opportunity. They just wonder what you're up to and they're willing to take your DVD merely to satisfy their curiosity."

"That doesn't seem right."

"Maybe not, but don't be offended. Ultimately, it's your fault."

"My fault? How's that?"

"It's your responsibility to qualify the prospect. By asking the right questions, and by reading the prospect's signals, you should be able to tell if a prospect's interest is genuine."

"But what questions do I ask? How do I qualify the prospect? How will I know if the interest is real?"

"Slow down Turbo. Don't *you* go pathologically curious on me," he teases. "I already mentioned some resources that answer most of those questions. Check them out and we'll discuss them another time. Learn to crawl, before you walk; learn to walk, before you run."

"Okay," you reply, compliant, but not really satisfied.

"Sooner or later, you'll hand a disc or magazine to someone who accepts it out of nothing more than curiosity. When you check back with them, the lack of interest will be apparent. Now, tell me how this relates to rejection."

"This one is easy. The prospect isn't rejecting anything. He was merely satisfying his curiosity."

"Precisely. And once his curiosity is satisfied, he's done."

"Isn't it possible for the DVD or magazine to pique genuine interest?"

"Yes, that's a very astute question. It is possible and, occasionally, it does happen. Keep in mind the other traits that come with pathological curiosity. These same folks tend to be highly analytical and overly cautious. Sometimes, these prospects will get stuck analyzing and never move beyond that point. I call this Analysis Paralysis. Sometimes, his cautious nature causes the prospect to doubt the information you present. And finally, in extreme cases, you may not even get the point of even offering a disc to the curious, analytical, cautious type."

"What do you mean?"

"I mean, that in extreme cases, overly cautious prospects can unleash a torrent of questions right then and there. It's rare and you can minimize the chances of this through effective communication. You can even prepare for it by having a few appropriate responses at the ready," he adds to reassure you.

"But we're not going to cover those now, are we," a hint of disappointment in your voice.

"Nope."

"Let me guess—I can read about communication on my own, and, right now, we're going to stay focused on the topic of rejection..."

"You got it," he confirms.

He continues with, "The bottom line is that some people will be curious, but not genuinely interested. Some will analyze your information with too much skepticism to accept the good parts. Some are so cautious by nature, that their unconscious defense mechanisms will keep your offer at arm's length."

"And the point is that none of them are rejecting me," you add.

"And why not?"

"Because their responses reflect the way they view the world. They approach everything with curiosity, caution or skepticism. They are not rejecting me in particular."

"Wow. Well said. Maybe I should be the one taking notes."

"Anything else I need to know about this response?"

"Yes. Just like we discussed before, your opportunity is not on trial. The prospecting encounter is not the time or place to defend your company or your offer. Nor is it the time or place to start answering questions. You can never say enough to get a 'yes', but it's all too easy to say enough to get a 'no'. I once heard it said like this: 'you can never wear 'em down to a yes.'

"Have you recognized any patterns in our discussion so far?"

"Several," and as you look down at your notes, you list them. "(1) In general, there is no need to fear rejection because I'm not the object of rejection. (2) Effective prospecting requires effective communication. (3) It is critical to have a working knowledge of human nature and the basic personality types."

"You're getting this lot quicker than I did. Now quit stalling," he teases again. "What's next on that list of yours?"

6. No thanks, I'm allergic to chocolate.

"This is another response that I only heard once."

"You won't hear it from many prospects either. In the past, it was much more common, but not so much any more. Care to guess how this response relates to prospecting?"

"Well, food allergies can be dangerous. When a restaurant patron identifies a specific food allergy, we take great pains to keep that ingredient well away from the patron. In terms of business, I'm not sure why a prospect would feel threatened by my offer much less, perceive it as dangerous."

"Yeah," he says, nodding. "This analogy is not as obvious as some of the others. It's actually pretty basic, though.

He continues on. "Our business model is not like other, more traditional, business models. In fact, when the industry first formed, it was completely unregulated. Not only did individuals not understand the concept, the government didn't know what to do with it either. This doesn't make the industry bad; it just makes it different. In the early days, a lot of people were distrustful of the idea. Many of them thought our business model was a scam. A few of them still do.

"In some cases they are right. New companies pop up all the time. And some small percentage of them, aren't necessarily a hundred percent legal. Some prospects, the uninformed ones, tend to paint all companies with the same brush, referring to them *all* as 'scams.' You'll never hear a prospect say, 'I'm allergic to your business model,' but every now and then, you may hear the 'S' word.

He finishes with, "Tell me how this relates to rejection."

Your rising confidence is obvious in your response. "Simple. The prospect is rejecting what he believes to be a scam. It has nothing to do with me personally."

"That's right. Now, as a person of integrity, you may feel the need to defend your business. After all, in a way, calling your business a scam comes pretty close to attacking your personal character. Most of the time, it's not worth the effort to offer a defense. Remember: professionals sort; amateurs convince— and you're not an amateur.

"I hear you, but can you give me more to go on?"

"What do you mean?"

"I know that our specific company is legit; it couldn't possibly be a scam, but I'm wondering if there are some points that I can use to bolster my confidence in the legitimacy of the industry in general?"

"Sure. You're catching on so fast, that I forget how new you are. I don't want to spend a lot of time on them, but I can zoom through a few points for you to ponder.

"Number one: Many name brands, household names, enjoy making their products available through multiple networking companies. At one time or another, manufacturers of soft drinks, high-end clothing, automobiles and just about everything in-between has been available through a business network. These companies have plenty of lawyers and plenty of smart marketing people. If it's legit enough for them, who are we to question it?

"Number two: consider the longevity of the industry. It's been around for decades. If the entire concept was questionable, it would be outlawed; not regulated.

"Number three: simple logic. If you are told the compensation plan works in a particular way, and then your check shows up for the correct amount, how can it be a scam? The company met its obligation and lived up to your expectation. Is that not the very definition of legitimate?

"I don't want to get bogged down on this point, but I did want to address your question. Does that give you some things to think about?"

"Definitely. I appreciate it. Those are the kinds of things I was looking for."

"Good. What response would you like to address next?"

You look back at the dwindling list of patron responses and read out the first one that isn't already crossed out.

7. I don't like chocolate chip cookies

"I couldn't believe it when I heard this one," you say.

"I know what you mean. I have trouble believing it when prospects tell me the same thing."

"Let me guess—this represents a patron saying, 'I don't like network marketing?'"

"Very good! That's exactly what it represents. It's not limited to network marketing though. It also applies to direct sales, and party plan opportunities, as do all the 'cookie lessons.'"

"I can see where this one is going. Is it okay if I take a stab at the summary?"

"Be my guest..."

"The prospect who says 'I don't like network marketing' is rejecting the business model, not the individual, like me, who is pursuing the business. Just like with the other lessons, there is no personal rejection to fear. How's that?"

"Perfect. Ready to move on?" he asks; never one to waste time.

"Before we do that, can you tell me why some people dislike our business model so much?"

"I suppose I could itemize a whole list of reasons, but the truth is that every one of them would boil down to one single explanation—ignorance. And I *don't* mean stupidity. Stupidity is the inability to learn, ignorance is simply having a lack of information. People who 'don't like' our business simply do not have all the facts. If people truly understood what we do, you and I wouldn't have to prospect them at all. We would just sit in the local coffee shop and interview applicants."

"Why do you say that? I mean, I believe that the business model is awesome, but I' can't really articulate why I believe it. I guess I've got my own share of ignorance too."

"Let me ask you, are you getting anything out of our visit today?"

"Absolutely!"

"So you feel like talking through the patron responses is helping your business more forward?"

"No question about it."

"Good. Now answer this: how much am I charging you for my time?"

"Uh, nothing...I hope," you say with the sudden realization that you don't have your credit card with you.

"That's right—nothing. I'm here to help you gain knowledge in the hope that you will use that knowledge to build a successful business. When you succeed, I succeed. The more you earn, the more I earn. That's how compensation works in our business model. Of course, I am taking a risk. If you decide to not succeed, then my compensation for helping you is forfeited.

And then he moves in to drive the point home. "Here's another question: how many people, besides me, stepped up and volunteered to sow knowledge, wisdom and time into your life without asking anything in return?"

"Uh...that would be *none*."

"And that is precisely what makes this business so awesome. Success in our profession requires one to serve first and receive later. The more you serve, the more you receive. Your compensation is directly proportional to the number of people you influence in a positive way. It's the Law of Sowing and Reaping in full force."

"That last saying sounds familiar...It's in one of the books I read—*The Go-Giver*, I believe," you say pleased with the recognition.

"It sure is.

"When I first read that, I thought, what a great concept. I had no idea that one day I'd be building a business based on the idea."

Bringing the conversation back around, he says, "You wanted to know how to articulate what makes our business so awesome. Does that help?"

"Boy, does it ever," you reply, nodding emphatically. "It's really pretty profound when you think about it."

"It *is* profound and I do think about it. Wait until you're on my side of the table. That's when the full significance of what we're doing strikes home. The reward defies words."

"Well, one thing's for sure—I won't ever be bothered by the 'I don't like network marketing' response. Once you understand the truth, it's a non-issue."

"It's the same for all the responses. Now, what's the next one?"

8. Do you have peanut butter instead?

"I thought this one was kinda' rude," you sneer with more than a little bit of attitude.

"Why do you say that?"

"Well, there I was offering a world-class dessert for free, and some yahoo has the gall to ask for something else—also for free."

"At least he was being honest with you. He wanted a cookie. He just didn't want the flavor you were offering."

"What was wrong with the chocolate chip cookies?"

"Not one thing. He just preferred something else. Why do you think there are so many different kinds of cookies? Different people have different preferences. Make sense?"

"So far."

"Well, there are a lot of different kinds of companies in our industry. Some people prefer tangible products; some prefer intangibles like services. Some are interested in health and well-being; others are more interested in travel. Me? As long as the product is valid, I'm more interested in the compensation plan. The bottom-line, though, is that no one company will appeal to everyone."

"In other words, different strokes for different folks?"

"Exactly."

"So what you're saying is that some prospects will be open to the idea of our business model, but not necessarily our company in particular."

"Bingo!"

"But ours is the best. Shouldn't I try to win them over?"

"That's a loaded question. There are too many variables to provide a simple answer that always applies. However, if you find that the prospect is already active with another company, leave him be. Never try to persuade someone to leave one company in order to join yours. We call that cross-recruiting. It's a predatory practice and you should refrain from it at all costs."

"But if ours in better…"

"It doesn't matter. How would you feel about someone cross-recruiting your team? Besides, if they're willing leave their current team now, they're willing leave yours later. You can waste a lot of time chasing those shadows."

"Okay, I get the point."

"How does this concept apply to rejection?" he prompts.

"The prospect is not rejecting me personally."

"What *is* the prospect rejecting?"

"The prospect is not actually rejecting *anything*. He is merely expressing the fact that he would be more interested in some other company."

"And the fear…"

"What fear?"

"Precisely," he nods. "Next…"

9. Can I get you to put one in a doggie bag for me?

"This was a common response that night, but I'm used to it. We serve large portions at the restaurant and lots of people ask for doggie bags."

"You'll hear it quite a bit when you prospect too."

"I will?"

"Yes, you will. Let me break it down for you, by way of a few questions…"

What is it with all the questions, you wonder. It seems as though your mentor is asking more than he's explaining. Surely, that can't be accurate though because if it is, how could you be learning so much?

"First question: Why do people ask for doggie bags?"

"In case they get hungry later?"

"You're asking, not telling. Are you unsure?"

"I guess I really don't know why people ask for doggie bags."

"Okay here's a hint: How much does the average dish cost in your restaurant?"

There is a lull in the conversation while you take a moment to think it through…

"Oh! It's because the patrons don't want to waste their money."

"You're on the right track. They are concerned about missing out on some part of the meal, which they paid good money for. They enjoyed the experience in your restaurant and they want to maximize that experience any way they can. The doggie bag is a souvenir of sorts. Am I making sense so far?"

"So far."

"Second question: Do you really believe that everyone who takes home a doggie bag actually eats the food it contains?"

"Probably not."

"I agree. I know that my spouse and I never do," he says. "I don't believe that very many people do actually eat the leftovers. It's the same way with prospects."

"I can't wait to hear this..."

And he doesn't keep you waiting.

"When you prospect properly, you create a positive experience for the prospect which can make quite an impact. This positive impact causes the prospect to place a high value on your offer which, in turn, motivates him to accept your DVD, often with sincere enthusiasm. Keep in mind why the restaurant patrons ask for doggie bags—because they want a souvenir of the experience. It's a very similar dynamic at work."

You ask him to repeat his last paragraph in order to make sure you get it captured in your notes.

"So my DVD's, magazines and sizzle call numbers are like souvenirs?"

"Yes. For some prospects, that's all they are."

"Well, if the prospect takes the information, it's a good thing, right?"

"Sure it is. Bear in mind, though, that's just the first step. You also want the prospect to look at, or listen to, the information. But not everyone will."

"In other words, not everyone will eat the leftovers..."

"Exactly. You will learn that some of the people you hand discs to will simply never look at them."

"And why is that?"

"Lot's of reasons. A friend of the prospect talks him out of the idea before he ever watches the DVD. The prospect talks himself out of the idea before he gets home that evening. After all, he doesn't know you from Adam. Maybe a dog ate the disc," he chuckles at his own joke. "We could go all day listing scenarios, but there's no sense in wasting the time. That's why Jim Rohm said..."

"Don't sign up for that class," you finish the quote.

"Right. Now, how does this relate to rejection?"

"Well...it wasn't me that got rejected; after all, he did take the disc. Plus, he never looked at the disc, so he really wasn't rejecting the information either."

"Good. And why didn't he look at the information? Why didn't he eat the leftovers," he asks, driving the point home.

"He took the disc because of the positive experience of the first encounter. We don't know why he didn't look at it."

"And..."

"And I refuse to sign up for that class," you say beaming.

"How many more of those responses do you have? You should be just about out of them."

You glance at your list in order to answer his question.

"Only four, but they're all things said by patrons who *did* take a cookie."

"Sometimes, 'yeses' can be deceiving. Give me an example."

10. My friend loves chocolate chip cookies. Is it okay if I take one for him?

"This one caught me off-guard. At first I didn't quite know what to say."

"How did you respond?"

"I gave him the cookie. Presumably, he took it to his friend," you answer.

"Care to guess how this one relates to prospecting?"

"Well...if the patron represents the prospect and if the cookie represents my DVD, then I suppose you're going to tell me that the prospect is going to take the disc and hand it to a friend of his."

"That's exactly what I'm going to tell you. Let's not blow this one out of proportion though—it's not exactly the most common scenario.

He continues...

"Let's say the prospect is named Jack and his best friend is Bobo."

"Okay."

58

"Let's also say that Bobo is a huge fan of our business model."

"Okay."

"How likely do you think it is that Bobo has approached Jack with an opportunity or two or three?"

"Very."

"You better believe it. And, right away, Jack recognizes your offer for what it is. Jack doesn't necessarily have a problem the business model, but in his mind, it 'just isn't his kinda thing.' Nevertheless, he and Bobo are good friends, and Jack knows that Bobo is always open to looking at 'those things."

"And…"

"And that's it. Jack thinks he's doing Bobo a favor by bringing the disc."

"Now there are different ways to handle this scenario and how to manage the follow-up is one important question, but we'll leave that to a future session. Right now, tell me how the 'can I take one to my friend' response applies to rejection.

"There is no rejection," you say it as more of a question than a statement.

"Correct. He didn't reject you—he referred you!"

"Another example of nothing to fear," spoken partly to yourself and partly aloud.

"After you get your mind around that, call out the next one.

11. How many of them can I have?

"This one caught me a bit off-guard too. My immediate thought was, 'You're a greedy little sucker aren't you?'"

"Heh, heh. What did you say out loud?"

"I said, 'You can have as many as you like. All we ask is that you take one at a time.'"

"That's a great response. You think pretty quick on your feet."

"Yeah, well, today I'm learning that, in prospecting, I need to be thinking ahead of time and not relying on haphazard, random things to say."

"Wise advice and that is a part of what we're doing here today. So let's get to the 'how many can I have' response."

"I'm ready," you acknowledge, pen poised.

"This one is less obvious than some of the others, but it does make me think of one prospecting scenario in particular. You're going to have times when you make an offer and the prospect just lights up. I mean they get some kind of excited. You see it in their expression, you hear it in their voice, and they tell you how they have 'been looking for something to come along' or perhaps they have 'been praying for some sort of relief.'"

"Really?"

"Oh, yeah. It's happened to me plenty of times," he confirms.

"That's cool! I can't wait for it to happen to me," your enthusiasm apparent.

"Trust me, it will."

"Well, there certainly isn't any rejection associated with that response!"

"Oh, there can be," he corrects you gently.

"But, how? If the prospect is so excited…"

"Extreme emotions can be short-lived. The prospect may not be so excited when you call to follow-up."

"Oh," you say, feeling dejected.

At that very moment, your mentor grins like a Cheshire cat staring at a fishbowl. Why do you suddenly feel like a lone goldfish in that bowl?

"See what I mean?" he asks. "You were all fired up when I described the excited prospect. When you learned things may not fare so well in the follow-up call, your emotion switched from enthusiasm to disappointment. Do you see how quickly people can switch emotions?"

"Yes. Wow. You're right. That's really something."

"Now don't jump off any buildings just yet. I'm not saying that excited prospects are always going to change tunes overnight. I'm just saying that you need to be prepared for the possibility because it does happen. I call these folks 'Match Heads.' Their emotions flare up initially, then, almost as quickly, subside and burn themselves out—leaving nothing but charred remains. This usually means that they went off in their enthusiastic ignorance and asked for a friend's opinion. And even that scenario can turn out good, but don't count on it.

"The bottom-line is that super-enthusiastic prospects may or may not change their tune by the time you call to follow-up. Just be prepared for either scenario."

You scribble hurriedly to finish your notes on the most recent point.

"Okay; got it," you say when you're ready to proceed.

"How does this response relate to rejection?" he asks.

"I'm not sure."

"Let me help you out. There is no rejection in either scenario because if the prospect remains excited, you move him to the next step. This means you communicated effectively and you qualified the prospect. His initial enthusiasm was sincere and he remained enthusiastic even through the follow-up call. Make sense?"

"Sure."

"If, on the other hand, he switches emotions, it's not because you did anything wrong. It's because he allowed outside influences to dictate his situation, in this case, to decline your offer and to stay where he is in life. He knows instinctively that he is letting down not only himself, but also the people he cherishes most. This is not a pleasant place to be. If you sense negative emotions during the follow-up call, that could very well be where they come from. The important thing to know is that he was not rejecting you. Consequently there is no rejection to fear."

"That makes sense."

"Two more right?" he asks.

"Yes. The next one is..."

12. Sure, I'll take one.

"I'm still confused by this one," you say.

"Why? It sounds positive."

"Yeah, but several patrons told me this and then they never took even one bite of the cookie."

"Well, now that does change things, doesn't it? It's almost as if the prospect says one thing while meaning something else entirely," he says, in his best analytical tone.

"Exactly! They said one thing all the while meaning something completely different."

"I wouldn't worry about it too much. As fast as you're learning, I don't expect you to get this response very many times; at least not from prospects."

"I don't follow..."

"It's pretty simple, really. These are the prospects that already know they're not interested. They only take the disc because they believe that's the quickest way to get you off their back."

"Off their back? I'm not going to be on anyone's back. Professional sort; amateurs convince."

"Correct, but you just learned that today. You know it consciously, but you may not believe it unconsciously; not yet. You will though. It's a simple matter of more understanding and some practice."

"Why does it matter what I believe unconsciously?"

"Because you unconscious mind is where your true beliefs reside and your actions will always follow your beliefs. In the case of prospecting, it's possible for the subconscious mind to actually sabotage a prospecting conversation."

"You're kidding."

"Not at all. I see it all the time. It happened to me when I first got started. Now, bear in mind that it's the subconscious mind doing the sabotage, and the subconscious mind can be exceedingly sneaky. The sabotage normally comes out in the form of negative body language and other unintentional behaviors. Speech is primarily a conscious behavior so usually the words you say are not affected."

"So how does all that affect the prospect?" you ask, fascinated.

"Profoundly, that's how. Your words are spoken consciously and the prospect hears them consciously. Likewise, your negative signals are given off unconsciously and that is how the prospect receives them. The net result is that you send a mixture of positive and negative messages. This is confusing to the prospect. And what did we say a few minutes ago? A confused mind does what?..."

You consult back to your notes and there it is—in the notes for "I'll have one later..."

"Nothing," you complete his sentence. "A confused mind does nothing."

"That's right. So, the prospect is confused, and what he or she wants, more than anything else, is to end the conversation. That's why they take the disc—to end the conversation. It was never about their interest in your offer."

"So, in this scenario there is rejection. In fact, I am the object of rejection."

"That's one way to put it, but it's more accurate to say that the prospect is rejecting his, or her, own confusion. Nevertheless, you did cause the confusion. So ultimately, the responsibility is yours.

He continues, "In some of today's lessons, we established that there isn't any rejection at all. But, the point is not whether there is any rejection in a particular prospect response. The point of the lessons is to remove the fear associated with rejection. Rejection is part of life; you have no control over that. How you respond to rejection—well—now that is completely under your control. Do you see my point?"

"So how do I deal with the rejection of giving someone a disc only to find out that they were merely trying to avoid me?"

"With confidence—confidence in the fact that you have all the information you need to eradicate any counter-productive beliefs hiding out in your subconscious mind. Employing this information brings your subconscious beliefs in line with your conscious knowledge, thus no more mixed signals—and none of the rejection that comes with them."

"And what information is that?"

"You did take notes, earlier, when I recommended some resources for you to check out, right."

"Yes, sir. Enough said," you say, determined to hit the web when you get home.

"Any more responses?"

"Just one," you reply. "And here it is…"

13. As a matter of fact, I would very much like a cookie.

"There didn't seem to be anything special about this response. I served the patrons cookies and they ate them," you explain.

"And they seemed to enjoy the cookies?"

"Yes, they did. Those were the patrons we were targeting with the dessert promotion. Some of them have already referred others to the restaurant so we know the strategy is working."

"And those are exactly the kind of prospects you are targeting with your business too. You make an offer to them, they accept your DVD, they consume the information and they like what they see. Next thing you know, they're sharing with others. That's when you know *our* strategy is working."

"That sounds easy enough," you respond.

"It's not complicated, if that's what you mean, but it does take some work. I want you to think about something..."

"Okay."

"How many responses, total, are on that list of yours?"

"Thirteen."

"A baker's dozen—how appropriate. Out of all those responses, how many represent responses that we hope hear from prospects?"

"One. Maybe two."

"And how many of them cause a legitimate fear of rejection?"

"None of them," you answer.

"You got it! Now, take a couple of minutes to review your notes and tell me what you've learned today."

"But I've learned so much. I'm not sure I can do it all justice in a couple of minutes?"

"I understand. Just list the highpoints."

You go back to the beginning of your notes and begin scanning for the underlined portions, reading them aloud as you go...

1. Seek out additional knowledge through worthwhile resources.
2. I will always know more than my prospects.
3. Don't make prospecting look like a chore.
4. The timing of major life-events has a profound effect on the prospect's response to my offer. This timing is completely out of my control.
5. Past experiences, especially negative ones, can cause a ~~patron~~ prospect to decline. It's not my responsibility to debate the point.
6. Sometimes, significant others have more influence over the prospect's response than I do.
7. Some prospects will take a tool even though they have no intention of seriously considering my offer.

8. Not all prospects appreciate my business model and it's not my responsibility to convince them otherwise.

9. Some prospects, for whatever reason, will be more attracted to another company; no need to try and sway them.

10. Not everyone who looks at a prospecting tool will be interested; that's just how it is.

11. There are a number of reasons why prospects might decline my offer, but none of them are a rejection of me personally.

12. When there is no rejection, there is no reason to fear.

With a big smile of approval, he says, "Nicely done. You took some great notes. I recommend you read through them a couple of times a week. And hang on to them. Who knows, maybe someday you'll write a book about them."

"That's funny. Who would read a book about this conversation?" you ask rhetorically.

"Well, we've gone through your list, so if you don't have any other questions, we're done. Next time, we'll talk about the follow-up process."

"Actually, I do have one more question…"

"Okay…fire away."

"When we first sat down today, you said the name of this lesson is "The Most Expensive Cookies in the World." The cookies I handed out in the restaurant the other night were free. So are the DVD's that I hand out to prospects. If I give them out for free, why do you call them 'expensive'?"

"I was hoping you'd ask about that. If you think about it, all the scenarios we covered today focus on the things prospects might say as you make an offer. In other words, these scenarios assume that you actually *do* make an offer. There might be times however, when you have an opportunity to make an offer, but for some reason or another, *don't*. So, here's a question for you: how can you tell if a prospect is interested if you don't ask?"

"I can't; not if I don't ask."

"That's right, you can't know if you don't ask. You see, nearly everyone you meet is a potential business superstar, and you could have them on your team—if you step out of your comfort zone to make an offer. But, if you don't make an offer, you will never know what could have been. If you think about it, *not* making an offer can be awfully expensive. The DVD's and tools you *don't* hand out can cost you a fortune. The bottom line is: the tools you don't offer could very well turn out to be...*The Most Expensive Cookies in the World*.

"Four things come not back: the spoken word, the sped arrow, the past life, the neglected opportunity."

-Arabian proverb

"Nothing is more expensive than a missed opportunity."

-H. Jackson Brown, Jr.

*A*fterword

Talk about being in the right place at the right time! The waiter in our story was at the right restaurant on the right night serving the right couple who just happened to offer a gift in the form of a book. As a result of reading that book (something many people would not have done), a relationship of mutual respect developed. This relationship, in turn, grew into a priceless mentorship. Good for the waiter. Oh, wait...that waiter is you! Wow! I hope you appreciate the circumstances that brought about this powerful turn of events.

Know what's even more impressive than this made-up version of your life? Your *real* life, that's what. Take a moment to ponder the people, the circumstances and the choices it took to bring about an introduction to your current business opportunity. Think about the fine thread that, every day, weaves your past into your present. For many of us, it's a thin thread indeed. And that thin thread continues to weave all the way into your future.

Now think about all the people you meet as you journey through life. Guess what? These people have their own thin threads weaving through *their* lives. And you, my friend, are on those threads! That's right. Any time your life intersects with that of someone else, the two of you have an opportunity to build that intersection into something significant. Unfortunately, these intersections, these random encounters if you will, typically never get pursued. Most end up discarded, carelessly tossed aside, with no second thought. How many times have you crossed paths with people who need and want the benefits of your business only to keep right on moving, forgetting to extend a business invitation until well after the encounter has passed? If you're like I used to be, it's all too often.

Even more tragic than discarding an intersection without thinking about it, is discarding one on purpose. I've been guilty of that too. I can remember times having a nice, albeit short, conversation with a total stranger. There I was telling myself all the reasons to make an offer, to prospect the person, but in the end, didn't. Ever been there? Sure you have.

For me, it was largely a fear of rejection. Until, that is, I began to learn the lessons of the cookies. And I didn't have the luxury of seeing all the lessons laid out on a shiny silver platter either. I had to learn them the old-fashioned way—one elusive ingredient at a time. I pray that you'll benefit from my experience.

Don't hold back; no need for manners here. Grab all the cookies you want. Stuff your mouth full. Come on—let's see those chipmunk cheeks of yours. And after you scarf down the last one, lick the chocolate off your fingers. When you're done with that, scoop up the crumbs and enjoy them too; don't stop until you've scraped up and finished off every last crumb from the platter and the floor alike. And if you make a habit of eating on the couch, well, you better dig behind the cushions too.

Even after the last cookie crumb is gone, you're still just getting started. There's a world full of other dishes you need to feast on, and I don't mean junk food. On the contrary, the feast

I'm referring to is one of good, clean wholesome information—information that infuses you with hope, confidence, influence, and a willingness to serve. I am, of course, referring to personal development—information designed to help you expand and reach you full potential; specialized knowledge about key aspects of human behavior, how to communicate effectively with different types of people, and about how to apply responsible influence.

Whether you graze or feast, this diet of personal development information will bolster an amazing brand of confidence—an overwhelming confidence against which no obstacle can prevail; not even close.

This process of consuming wholesome ingredients doesn't happen accidentally; just the opposite. If you partake of this mind-nourishing diet, it is because you make a deliberate choice to do so. And make no mistake—there are only two choices—to partake or not to partake. It's a classic case of all or nothing. This one choice is the difference between mediocrity and excellence. Choose excellence. Choose to partake of the good stuff. Choose to feast on personal development. Nothing else will suffice. Not even close.

Personal development is simple; locate some great information, grab a hold of it and then dig in with gusto. I don't care if you gobble it, gulp it, quaff it, poke it, snort it, sniff it, stuff it, swig it or swallow it whole, just get it down; somehow get it inside you. You might find that you enjoy the cuisine of personal development. Then again, if you're like I was in the beginning, you may find it a bit on the bland side. For me, personal development was an acquired taste. Over time, I learned to delight in every dish, to savor every sip. And if you have a sweet tooth, well, you can always chase the meal with a cookie.

With modern technology, personal development content comes in a variety of formats. Thankfully, most of them are more comfortable than poking and stuffing—more convenient too. You have CD's and MP3's for listening, DVD's and on-line videos for material which you prefer to watch and then there's always the good ol' standby technology—books, and today, even they are available in electronic formats.

There's no shortage of great personal development material. With only a cursory search on-line, you'll find a veritable cornucopia of dishes to choose from and they're all laid out in buffet fashion for your personal development enjoyment. You can eat as much as you want and you can eat as often as you want. You can have dessert first and you can ignore the broccoli altogether. No other spread can touch this one. Not even close. With so many yummy things to choose from, how do you know what to start with?

Check up-line. Chances are the leaders of your success team would be thrilled to provide a number of worthwhile recommendations. Some of your top leaders may even have original content of their own. If so, you probably ought to get your hands on some (of the content, not your team leaders) and wolf it down.

Being from the South, I'm partial to good ol' country cooking—you know—hearty meals of steak, potatoes, gravy and a variety of fresh vegetables, fried, of course; all washed down with lemonade or sweet tea. Now, *that's* good eatin'. No quiche or seltzer water for me. I have the same taste in personal development content—if I'm going to invest the time to munch a book, or chug on a forty-five minute audio, it better be filling, it better "stick to the ribs."

Having attended dozens of conventions and scores of seminars, having read a long and growing list of books, and having listened to well over a thousand audios, I've consumed a significant amount of personal development. You can't eat that much of anything without some it sticking to your ribs. And of all the personal development meals I've eaten, several stand out as remarkable.

Some of them are remarkable because of the degree to which they affected my mindset. These include satisfying dishes about self-talk, the power of language, transforming obstacles into motivations, giver's gain and incorporating personal values into everyday activities.

The others are remarkable because of the contributions they made to my external skills. These include a smorgasbord of high-impact content; things like effective communication, relating to a wide range of people, bringing value into the lives of others and the list goes on.

Some readers are hungry for a mind-nourishing diet that can satisfy an extraordinary appetite. These readers are encouraged to visit here for a list of yummy, mind-nourishing dishes. They may not all be as scrumptious as world-famous chocolate chip cookies, but I guarantee they'll all stick to your ribs. If you don't like my list, get one from somewhere else because there is no substitute for nourishing your mind. Nothing else will suffice.

Above all else—remember the cookies. That way, fear of rejection won't stand a chance.

Not even close.

Bon appétit.

"Stressed spelled backward is desserts. Coincidence? I think not."

Now...someone pass me a cookie.

About the Author

Russ McNeil didn't exactly enter the world of team building with the skills necessary to be an instant success. With an overbearing personality, a disinterested warm market and a genuine fear of approaching strangers, he had significant obstacles to overcome. And overcome them he did. Through trial, error, diligence and determination, he eventually mastered the art of situational prospecting.

It was a successful mentor who initially recognized Russ's uncanny skill of connecting with complete strangers. At this mentor's urging, Russ found himself on stage, teaching the fundamentals of situational prospecting. Those early experiences of teaching the subject to live audiences underscored a huge void in our profession: As a whole, our profession is exceedingly good about telling reps *what* to do, but not so hot about telling them *how* to do it. There is very little training on how to meet, engage and make an offer to people you encounter randomly during the course of everyday life. The purpose of Russ's content is to fill that void. Through his conversational presentation style, appealing sense of humor, and real-world experience, the author brings readers and audiences to new levels of understanding on the subject of prospecting.

Russ really did grow up in the South, he really was raised on a good ol' fashioned menu and he really doesn't know the first thing about cooking. He would have significant difficulty merely following a recipe, much less writing a one—about *food* that is. Some people, however, think he's fairly adept at writing recipes for sales training, especially with respect to prospecting.

The important thing, though, is not how yummy his recipes taste, but rather how satisfying they are to his audiences. Russ's content is not about him. It's about you. To that end, he shares wisdom and real-world experience with you in a way that makes the content easy to digest, easy to implement, and easy to pass on to others. Hopefully, you found this book satisfying. Hopefully, it will stick to your ribs. And if not, well, maybe—just maybe—you should go back for seconds and eat read another helping.

Russ lives in North Texas with his wife of 25⁺ years, three sons and Milo, a beagle who excels at prospecting rabbits. If you wish to contact him (Russ that is, not Milo), to comment on his work or subscribe to his complimentary newsletter, you may do so through www.AhaUniversity.com, or email him directly at AhaUniversity@gmail.com.

Appendix A

More cookies, more lessons...

When you do on-line research for a book, especially when you're sifting for things like quotes, you run across all sorts of "unusual" flavors. Very few of them actually belong in the recipe of your work, but every now and then, you discover an unexpected spice or some tasty morsel that's simply too yummy to leave out. The poem below is one such ingredient. It even comes with a few great lessons. Try not to make a pig of yourself.

The Cookie Thief

by Valerie Cox

A woman was waiting at an airport one night
With several long hours before her flight
She hunted for a book in the airport shop
Bought a bag of cookies and found a place to drop
She was engrossed in her book but, happened to see
That the man beside her as bold as could be,
Grabbed a cookie or two from the bag between
Which she tried to ignore to avoid a scene
She munched cookies and watched the clock
As this gutsy cookie thief diminished her stock
She was getting more irritated as the minutes ticked by
Thinking "If I wasn't so nice I'd blacken his eye"
With each cookie she took, he took one too
And when only one was left she wondered what he'd do

With a smile on his face and a nervous laugh
He took the last cookie and broke it in half
He offered her half as he ate the other
She snatched it from him and thought "Oh brother!
This guy has some nerve and he's also rude
Why he didn't even show any gratitude"
She had never known when she had been so galled
And sighed with relief when her flight was called
She gathered her belongings and headed for the gate
Refusing to look back at the thieving ingrate
She boarded the plane and sank in her seat
Then sought her book which was almost complete
As she reached in her baggage she gasped with surprise
There was her bag of cookies in front of her eyes
"If mine are here…" she moaned with despair
"Then the others were his and he tried to share"
Too late to apologize she realized with grief
That she was the rude one, the ingrate, the thief.

On the surface, this poem is fun, but it also contains some great lessons for team builders…

- **Don't horde your cookies.** If the woman had offered to share her cookies, it would have been a very different poem. You have something worth sharing too, but if you keep your business to yourself, you won't enjoy how it ends either. Share your cookies at every opportunity. Look for occasions to hand out a free sample, a delicious DVD or savory sizzle call.

- **Be careful what stories you tell yourself**. The entire misunderstanding came about because of the woman's misguided assumption about the man. She made up an entire story in which she relegated the man to the role of thief. Team-builders often make up and tell themselves stories about prospects: He's too busy, too successful, she's too educated, too sophisticated, and the list goes on. Stop doing that! Things are not always as they appear. You don't have enough information to rewrite the prospect's story. Doing so is unfair—to you and the prospect.

- **Strangers can be nice too**. The man in the poem was actually a nice guy. He was perfectly willing to share his cookies even though the woman, a stranger, never asked. How generous is that? He might be just the kind of person to go out and share an opportunity. Every day, you encounter strangers too, people—nice, generous people— whom you don't know (yet!). Don't rule them out.

- **Take time to engage.** Had the woman taken time to engage the man in a casual, friendly conversation, the entire misunderstanding would have been averted. People are starved for conversation. They just don't want to be the one to start it. Prospecting requires conversation and conversation requires you to engage. After all, strangers are looking for opportunities too.

- **Admit your mistakes.** The woman realized her mistake. Unfortunately, it was too late to make amends. Be humble. Recognize and admit your mistakes. This advice is a crucial component of effective people skills. And make no mistake—when it comes to prospecting, effective people skills are a necessity, not a luxury.

Appendix B

Why engineers shouldn't write recipes...

What follows, is a recipe for chocolate chip cookies developed by an engineer (much like me, before I began my recovery with EA):

Inputs

   a) 532.35 cm^3 gluten

   b) 4.9 cm^3 NaHCO$_3$

   c) 4.9 cm^3 refined halite

   d) 236.6 cm^3 partially hydrogenated tallow triglyceride

   e) 177.45 cm^3 crystalline C$_{12}$H$_{22}$O$_{11}$

   f) 177.45 cm^3 unrefined C$_{12}$H$_{22}$O$_{11}$

   g) 4.9 cm^3 methyl ether of protocatechuic aldehyde

   h) 2 calcium carbonate-encapsulated avian albumen-coated protein

   i) 473.2 cm^3 theobroma cacao

   j) 236.6 cm^3 de-encapsulated legume meats (sieve size #10)

Processing

1. To a 2-L jacketed round reactor vessel (reactor #1) with an overall heat transfer coefficient of about 100 Btu/F-ft2-hr, add ingredients a), b) and c) with constant agitation.

2. In a second 2-L reactor vessel with a radial flow impeller operating at 100 rpm, add ingredients d), e), f), and g) until the mixture is homogenous.

3. To reactor #2, add ingredient h), followed by three equal volumes of the homogenous mixture in reactor #1.

4. Additionally, add ingredients i) and j) slowly, with constant agitation. Take care at this point in the reaction to control any temperature rise that may be the result of an exothermic reaction.

5. Using a screw extrude attached to a #4 nodulizer, place the mixture piece-meal on a 316SS sheet (300 x 600 mm). Heat in a 460°K oven for a period of time that is in agreement with Frank & Johnston's first order rate expression (see JACOS, 21, 55), or until golden brown.

6. Once the reaction is complete, place the sheet on a 25°C heat transfer table, allowing the product to come to thermal equilibrium.

Pretty tough to follow, isn't it? Doesn't sound particularly appetizing does it? This recipe reminds me of my prospecting in the early days.

Prospecting is like baking chocolate chip cookies. If you want the prospect to follow along, if you want to keep the prospect engaged, you must communicate clearly and use appetizing ingredients. Now, that you've seen how not to do it, move on the next appendix.

Ingredients

a) Milk
b) Baking soda
c) Salt
d) Butter
e) Sugar
f) Unrefined sugar
g) Vanilla extract
h) Eggs
i) Cocoa
j) Shelled nuts

Appendix C

Russ's special recipe for blue-ribbon prospecting

Pages 17 and 18 describe the most outrageously delicious cookies ever baked. A recipe like that really stands out. If you knew how to bake like that, people would come from miles around. Wouldn't it be great if your prospecting approach was that irresistible? Well, it can be. You just need to know the recipe.

Referring back the description on page 17:

- Butterscotch—not in every bite; sporadic, light humor
- Chocolate-semi-sweet; good people skills, positive demeanor
- Peanut butter—smooth, creamy; relaxed & laid back
- Crunchy crust—thick skin; ready for 'no'
- Chewy center—soft; servant's attitude
- Cinnamon—compliments other flavors; modeling behavior style
- Mystery flavor—"The Secret Ingredient"

Mix these ingredients vigorously and thoroughly with personal development then bake them in the heat of real-world practice for just the right amount of time. You'll know when they're done.

For the specific details of this recipe, including the "The Secret Ingredient" of prospecting, check out the author's first book, _Prospecting Rules_. It addresses every aspect of prospecting from start to finish; what to say, when to say it, how to say it and even how _not_ to say it; from how to start a conversation to how to ask for the prospect's phone number. Ever wonder what to say when you follow-up? Ever want to know how to prevent no-shows? Now you can know all this and much, much more. And it's all in one easy-to-read, fun-filled, practical, guide. Discover more at the link above.

References

Souba, W (2006). "The Inward Journey of Leadership", 'Journal of Surgical Research', 131 (163).

Prospecting Rules!

A small sample of actual reader comments...

"Prospecting problems? Here is your answer!"
"It's Practical!!!"
"Get ready to laugh and learn."
"One Word : Powerful"
"Become Fearless!"

What to say, how to say it, and when to say it.
Never again struggle for the words to use.
To discover more click this page or visit ProspectingRules.com

Lessons from the Ark

A small sample of actual reader comments...

"A breath of fresh air!"
"Life changing. A game-changer!"
"...packed with valuable information..."
"Hugely entertaining"
"Dozens of ways to attract your ideal customer."

Attracting a steady stream of quality prospects – the pros
do it, now you can too. This book explains how in a fun
format that you will never forget!

Also available:

- _Prospecting with Purpose_, Russ's complimentary ezine
- _The Bodaciously Colossal Book of Business Quotations_ *(also complimentary)*

And coming soon...

- _Sticks and Stones_
- _Prospecting Matters_

To discover more, visit www.AhaUniversity.com.

<u>*Notes*</u>

"I missed 100% of the shots I never took." -Wayne Gretzky

Notes

"I missed 100% of the shots I never took." -Wayne Gretzky

Lightning Source UK Ltd.
Milton Keynes UK
UKOW03f0607081113

220645UK00002B/19/P